THE MINISTERIAL IDENTITY OF THE DEACON

Deacon William T. Ditewig, Ph.D.

 Publications

Cover and book design by Mary E. Bolin.

The Scripture quotations contained herein are from the
New Revised Standard Version Bible, copyright © 1989 by
the Division of Christian Education of the National Council
of the Churches of Christ in the U.S.A. Used by permission.

©2015 Saint Meinrad Archabbey
All Rights Reserved

ISBN 978-0-87029-678-9
Library of Congress 2015934755

Published by Abbey Press Publications
1 Hill Drive St. Meinrad, IN 47577
Printed by Abbey Press in the United States of America.
www.abbeypresspublications.com

For Diann, with all my love.

Contents

Foreword 3

What IS "Ministerial Identity"? 5

Initiation and Ordination:
    The Twin Pillars of Diaconal Identity 15

Discipleship and Apostleship 25

Deacons and Their States of Life:
    The Context of Identity 35

Ministerial Identity: It's All About Relationships.................. 45

Foreword by His Eminence Donald Cardinal Wuerl, Archbishop of Washington

In my nearly three decades as a bishop, I have had the wonderful privilege of ordaining many deacons, priests, and a fair number of bishops. For me, this is always a profoundly spiritual experience, realizing that it is precisely in the laying on of hands and the outpouring of the Holy Spirit that a unique and special configuration to Christ is taking place in the one being ordained.

Given the deep truth in the maxim, *lex orandi, lex credendi*, the prayer of the Church manifests the faith of the Church, I often use as a point of meditation the Rites of Ordination for all three—bishop, priest, and deacon— that are meant to guide the ordaining bishops' homily at the ordination itself.

Here we find in the Ordination of Deacons a rich vein of appreciation of the Church's ancient heritage, profound theology, and also current post-conciliar catechesis. It should not be surprising, given the nature of the diaconate, that both in the ritual and in the *Catechism of the Catholic Church,* the emphasis is on the service element of the diaconate. But the very incorporation of all three ordination ceremonies into one book of rites makes very clear the relationship of all three Holy Orders.

It is precisely the distinction of the three orders and yet their profound relationship that is the starting point for Deacon William Ditewig in this short, but well thought out consideration of the ministerial identity of the deacon. This challenging work is intended not to reach doctrinal conclusions, but to encourage deeper study of the diaconal ministry.

Deacon Ditewig asserts that ministerial identity is all about relationships. He offers insightful observations that ask the reader to envision a diaconate where all of the multi-layered relationships are experienced in such a way that the deacon is fully energized not only to carry out his ministerial obligations, but to do so in a communion of ministry that touches the whole Church.

In this age of the New Evangelization and ministerial discipleship, the diaconate is a providential blessing; and, the more it is understood and lived to its fullness, the more the Church of Christ is served.

CHAPTER I

What IS "Ministerial Identity"?

Theologian John Ford, along with others, has pointed out the rather imprecise uses of the term "ministry."[1] The word itself comes from the Latin *ministerium* which in turn translates from the Greek *diakonia*: "service." If the terms are not qualified in some way, it can be hard to sort out just what kind of "ministry" or "service" we're talking about. Consider just a couple of quick examples. Government officials are often referred to as "ministers," for example. In diplomatic service, ambassadors and legates are likewise called ministers. Within the world of the church, ministers are those who conduct religious "services" and provide related "services" to those they "serve." Prior to the Second Vatican Council, the term "ministry" was generally associated with clergy of religions other than the Catholic Church: those folks had ministers, while we Catholics had priests, sisters, and brothers.

With regard to deacons, whose very name means "servants," it is interesting that one of the early patristic sources on the diaconate observed that "deacons are not ordained to the priesthood, but into service to the bishop [*non ad sacerdotium sed in ministerio episcopi*], to do that which he commands."[2] Unlike some of the above definitions, here we find a specific qualification and precision. This service of the deacon was very specific: whatever the bishop commanded. Only a couple of hundred years later, as structures of Christian ministry were evolving, that phrase was shortened, and the specific reference to the bishop was removed. Now it was simply said that "deacons are not ordained to the priesthood, but to service [*non ad sacerdotium sed ad ministerium*]."[3] That service, that ministry, could now take a wide variety of forms.

While the forms of ministry associated with the Catholic deacon are many and varied, they are of secondary importance to us in this brief reflection on the ministerial identity of the deacon. What we are looking for is the foundation upon which the deacon's service rests.

Identity

Hamlet had it right: "To be, or not to be?" That really is the question.

What does it mean to be? What does it mean to be a particular person in God's creation? In this book, we will reflect on the specific question of what it means to be a deacon ordained for service by the Catholic Church. Often, when we speak about ministry in the Church, we hear about the functions being performed: lectors "read," Extraordinary Ministers of Holy Communion "distribute," catechists "catechize," and deacons, well… "deacon." But the real question is not "what do we do?" but "who are we when we do it?"

As Christians, we look to Christ as the model of ministry. He taught; but, many other people were also teaching. Christ healed the sick; but, there were other healers, other prophets, and other religious leaders all around. What made Christ's teaching, healing, prophesying, so unique? It was not *what* he was doing as much as *who* He was as he did it! "They were astounded at his teaching, because he spoke with authority" (Luke 4:32). Christ's actions had authority because of who he was: "...the Messiah, the Son of the Living God" (Matthew 16:16). As disciples of Christ, the same can be said of us. <u>The various forms of our service rest on the solid foundation of who we are as followers and imitators of Christ.</u>

Before going deeper into this relationship, let's put it into perspective. All kinds of people do many of the same things that we do, but they do them out of a different "identity;" their actions flow from a different foundation. Catholics are, of course, not the only people who serve; religious people are not the only people who care and act with compassion and generosity! Let me give an example.

Many years ago, I was asked to be a part of a panel of religious leaders addressing a large group of hospice volunteers. I was the Catholic member of the panel, along with a rabbi and a Lutheran minister. Our task was to give the participants some sense of the traditions of our respective faiths with regard to death and dying. Before we began, the three of us decided that we should find out the religious orientations of the audience. The pastor asked how many people identified themselves as members of Protestant churches. Only a handful of people raised their hands. Even fewer identified themselves as Catholic, so the rabbi thought he had us both beat, but no one there identified themselves as Jewish. In other words, out of the nearly one hundred people in attendance, fewer than 25% were there because of particular religious convictions. When we asked why they were involved in hospice—what motivated them to do that—one woman spoke up that it was simply the right thing to do—not from any particular religious perspective, but simply because human goodness and concern demanded it. Their "ministerial identity" was not based on religious discipleship, but a sense of civic responsibility and generosity.

So we come back to our fundamental question: what does it mean *to be* a deacon?

Specifically, what does it mean *to be* a deacon of the Catholic Church? Not, "what do deacons do?" but "who are deacons?" It has become almost cliché to hear deacons say, "It's not about what we do, but about who we are." Exactly. But we need to examine that ministerial (diaconal) identity more closely.

Baptism

It all starts with baptism.

When a deacon candidate is called to ordination, according to the instructions in the liturgical books, he is to vest in an alb. Think about that for a moment. The alb—the long white robe worn by a variety of ministers, lay and ordained—is the foundational vestment we wear. Altar servers in many locations wear them. Newly baptized adults wear them. Bishops, deacons, and presbyters wear them. Even the pope wears them. The alb is not a clerical vestment; by that, I mean that it is not a vestment worn only by the clergy. The significance of the alb is found in the fact that it represents the white garment given to us at our baptism. I sometimes think it would be wonderful to see every baptized person come to Sunday Mass dressed in albs. What a striking way to show each other that we are a community of the baptized!

It is over this foundation (i.e. the baptismal garment) that we who are ordained place the vestments unique to our office: the stole and dalmatic for the deacon, the stole and chasuble for the presbyter and bishop (although sometimes the bishop will wear both the dalmatic and the chasuble on solemn celebrations). So, the first element of the ministerial identity of any Christian is found in the waters of baptism.

In the waters of baptism we are immersed into the very life of the Trinity, filled with and consecrated by the Holy Spirit. Anointed with Sacred Chrism, we are charged with the words: "God the Father of our Lord Jesus Christ has freed you from sin, given you a new birth by water and the Holy Spirit, and welcomed you into his holy people. He now anoints you with the chrism of salvation. As Christ was anointed Priest, Prophet, and King, so may you live always as a member of his body, sharing everlasting life."

There it is: by baptism, we join in Christ's own identity as priest, prophet, and king.

I have always been humbled and challenged by part of a homily by the great Fourth Century bishop, Augustine of Hippo:

> For you I am a bishop; with you, after all, I am a Christian. The first is the name of an office undertaken, the second a name of grace; the first means danger, the second salvation. Finally, as if in the open sea, I am being tossed about by the stormy activity involved in the first; but as I recall by whose blood I have been redeemed, I enter a safe harbor in the tranquil recollection of the second; and thus while toiling away at my own proper office, I take my rest in the marvelous benefit conferred on all of us in common.[4]

In the following chapters, we will look more closely at the sacramental foundations of the deacon's ministerial identity, beginning with the Sacraments of Initiation and the Sacrament of Holy Orders.

For Reflection

1. How do our actions in service flow from our "being," our "identity" as disciples of Christ?

2. How does this identity as a Christian find expression in our service? In other words, what difference does it make? As discussed above, even people acting simply out of a sense of civic responsibility can do many of the same things people of faith do; so what difference does faith make in our own ministries?

Notes

[1] John Ford, "Ministries in the Church," in *The Gift of the Church: A Textbook on Ecclesiology in Honor of Patrick Granfield, OSB*, Peter C. Phan, ed. (Collegeville: Liturgical Press, 2000), 293-314, especially 293-294.

[2] Burton Scott Easton, trans. and ed., *The Apostolic Tradition of Hippolytus: Translated into English with Introduction and Notes* (Cambridge: University Press, 1934), 38-39.

[3] Joseph W. Pokusa, "A Canonical-Historical Study of the Diaconate in the Western Church" (JCD diss., Catholic University of America, 1979), 73, n. 41, citing *Concilia Galliae AD 314-AD 506, Corpus Christianorum, Series Latina*, vol. 148, ed. C. Munier (Turnholti: Typographi Brepols Editores Pontificii, 1963), 148-175, 181.

[4] St. Augustine, *Sermo* 340, 1: *PL* 38, 1483.

Chapter II

Initiation and Ordination: The Twin Pillars of Diaconal Identity

Sacraments of Initiation

The Sacraments of Baptism, Confirmation (called *chrismation* in the Eastern Catholic Churches), and Eucharist are collectively referred to as the "Sacraments of Initiation." It is already the established pattern in most Eastern Catholic Churches to celebrate all three sacraments together, usually in infancy. In the West, however, we frequently celebrate these sacraments at different times, although the norm is actually to celebrate them together. In the Latin Church, this has been the case since the re-introduction of the renewed catechumenate called for by the

Second Vatican Council in its *Constitution on the Sacred Liturgy* (*Sacrosanctum Concilium*).

I bring this up because the mystery of Christian initiation holds the key to our fundamental identity as a servant people, a servant Church. Here again, Vatican II holds the key for our reflection:

> It is through the sacraments and the exercise of the virtues that the sacred nature and organic structure of the priestly community is brought into operation. Incorporated in the Church through baptism, the faithful are destined by the baptismal character for the worship of the Christian religion; reborn as sons of God they must confess before men the faith which they have received from God through the Church. They are more perfectly bound to the Church by the sacrament of Confirmation, and the Holy Spirit endows them with special strength so that they are more strictly obliged to spread and defend the faith, both by word and by deed, as true witnesses of Christ. Taking part in the Eucharistic sacrifice, which is the fount

and apex of the whole Christian life, they offer the Divine Victim to God, and offer themselves along with It.[5]

Look at the call to ministry described and, in particular, the call to evangelization. Notice the strong note of obligation expressed in the passage. Through baptism, we are "destined" for worship; we "must confess" before all the faith we have received. Through the Sacrament of Confirmation and the "special strength" received from the Holy Spirit, we are "more strictly obliged" to spread and defend the faith. Finally, through initiation into the Eucharist—"the fount and apex" of Christian life—we all exercise our baptismal priesthood by offering Christ (and our selves, united with Christ) to the Father. With this in mind, the *Catechism of the Catholic Church* observes, "Baptism, Confirmation, and Eucharist are sacraments of Christian initiation. They ground the common vocation of all Christ's disciples, a vocation to holiness and to the mission of evangelizing the world. They confer the graces needed for the life according to the Spirit during this life as pilgrims on the march towards the homeland."[6]

Years before the promulgation of the *Catechism*, in *Christifideles Laici* ("The Vocation and the Mission of the Lay Faithful in the Church and in the World"), Pope Saint John Paul II taught:

> Communion and mission are profoundly connected with each other, they interpenetrate and mutually imply each other, to the point that communion represents both the source and the fruit of mission: communion gives rise to mission and mission is accomplished in communion. It is always the one and the same Spirit who calls together and unifies the Church and sends her to preach the Gospel "to the ends of the earth" (Acts 1:8).[7]

All of this applies, therefore, to each and every initiated Christian. The ordained, including us deacons, express this identity every time we put on our alb, the white garment of our baptism. This is why the Congregation for Catholic Education, in its 1998 document on the formation of deacons, begins its listing of "theological reference points" with the following: "First of all we must consider the diaconate, like every other Christian identity, from within the Church which is understood as a mystery of Trinitarian communion in missionary tension."[8] Immersed into the life of the Trinity and sealed with the Holy Spirit into a participation in the community of Christ, our identity as Christian disciples is established.

The Sacrament of Holy Orders

If our sacramental initiation is what calls us all to service, then what does ordination add to our ministerial identity? Once again, we turn to the Second Vatican Council for insight.

Chapter Three of *Lumen Gentium* addresses the hierarchical nature of the Church and, in particular, focuses on the ordained ministries of bishop, presbyter, and deacon. The first words of the chapter read:

> For the shepherding and constant growth of the People of God, Christ the Lord instituted in His Church a variety of ministries, which work for the good of the whole body. For those ministers, who are endowed with sacred power, serve their

brethren, so that all who are of the People of God, and therefore enjoy a true Christian dignity, working toward a common goal freely and in an orderly way, may arrive at salvation.[9]

As an introduction to the subject of the ordained ministries, these words are invaluable to us. The purpose of the ordained is to shepherd, to nurture the "constant growth of the People of God... [working] for the good of the whole body." The ordained receive "sacred power" to serve others. The idea of shepherding certainly evokes pastoral servant-leadership and the identification of Christ as the Good Shepherd. Those in ordained ministry find their model of service in that Good Shepherd, himself.

CCC 1581

Ordination confers a sacred power to help the ordinand carry out the demands of ministry. The *Catechism* points out that ordination "configures the recipient to Christ by a special grace of the Holy Spirit so that he may serve as Christ's instrument for his Church. By ordination, one is enabled to act as a representative of Christ, Head of the

Church, in his triple office of Priest, Prophet, and King."[10]

It is no coincidence that in both the Sacrament of Baptism, and in the Sacrament of Holy Orders, we read of Christ's role as priest, prophet, and king. And so, the ministerial identity of the deacon is initiated and confirmed, nurtured through the Eucharist, and then further empowered and focused through Holy Orders. Specifically, it can be said that what ordination conveys is a sense of servant-leadership for the rest of the community, as defined and described by the order to which a person is ordained. In the *Directory for the Ministry and Life of Permanent Deacons*, the Congregation for the Clergy states, "The origin of the diaconate is the consecration and mission of Christ, in which the deacon is called to share. Through the imposition of hands and the prayer of consecration, he is constituted a sacred minister and a member of the hierarchy. This condition determines his theological and juridical status in the Church" (1).

A bishop receives full responsibility for shepherding the People of God in his charge.

And in that ministry, he is assisted by deacons and presbyters, who participate in lesser ways in the ministerial identity of the bishop:

> Bishops, therefore, with their helpers, the priests and deacons, have taken up the service of the community, presiding in place of God over the flock, whose shepherds they are, as teachers for doctrine, priests for sacred worship, and ministers for governing.[11]

While the bishop is the "prime" minister over a diocese, priests and deacons assist the bishop in the service of shepherding the People of God.

It is upon these twin sacramental pillars—sacramental initiation and ordination—that the ministerial identity of the deacon is founded, and upon which his functions develop. In a very real sense, the discipleship of Christ into which the deacon was initiated is then paired with the further call to apostleship, as the deacon is ordained into the apostolic ministry of the bishop.

For Reflection

1. How does the twin sacramentality of initiation and ordination find expression in your own life and ministry?
2. In your own life, how do the sacraments of initiation ground your ministry as deacon?
3. Since the apostolic ministry involves an exercise of servant-leadership in shepherding the community, how is this leadership expressed in your own ministry?

Notes

[5] *Lumen Gentium*, #11.
[6] *Catechism of the Catholic Church*, #1533.
[7] John Paul II, post-synodal Apostolic Exhortation, "The Vocation and the Mission of the Lay Faithful in the Church and in the World" (*Christifideles Laici*) (December 30, 1988) (Washington, D.C.: United States Catholic Conference, 1988), #32.
[8] Congregation for Catholic Education, "Basic Norms for the Formation of Permanent Deacons" (Vatican City: Libreria Editrice Vaticana, 1998), #4.
[9] *Lumen Gentium*, #18.
[10] *Catechism of the Catholic Church*, #1581.
[11] *Lumen Gentium*, #20.

Chapter III

Discipleship and Apostleship

(annotation: Discipleship → FROM SACRAMENTS OF INITIATION; Apostleship → FROM ORDINATION)

"All authority in heaven and on earth has been given to me. Go therefore and make disciples of all nations, baptizing them in the name of the Father and of the Son and of the Holy Spirit, and teaching them to obey everything that I have commanded you."[12]

We have seen how our sacramental initiation immerses us into the life of the Trinity and the mission of Christ: Priest, Prophet, and King. Ordination then configures the disciple in a more particular way to Christ; and the Church, as we have also seen, refers to this as "apostolic ministry." In this chapter, then, we will reflect on this relationship between the discipleship shared by all baptized followers of Christ, and the apostleship to which some disciples are also called.

Terminology

A *disciple* is one who learns… a "discerner," if you will. In general usage, we often speak of a teacher and her disciples: not out of any particular religious meaning, but simply that these students are following and learning from that teacher; they could be studying anything from mathematics or physics to English literature or history. The Latin word for teacher is *magister*, from which we derive the English word, "master." We find "master" used in reference to teachers ("schoolmaster", for example, or simply "master" in many English-speaking schools). A person who has received a "Master's Degree" was at one time considered ready and qualified to teach the subject in question. So, within education, we often speak of masters and disciples.

Of course, these words are also found in the specific context of religion: followers of a particular religious teacher, leader, guru, or evangelist are often called disciples of that "master." Even within various cults, we find the language of disciples and master. Within

Christianity, however, these terms take on much more precise meanings.

The Master is, of course, Jesus. He is frequently referred to in the Gospels by the Hebrew term *rabbi*, "my teacher." Those who associate themselves with Jesus, who are following him and learning from him, are his disciples. It is within this context that we consider the verses with which we opened this chapter. This is, of course, the "Great Commission" given to Christ's followers immediately before his ascension to the Father. They are told "go" and make disciples of all nations. They are given a very specific mission from their Risen Master: they are sent forth. In Greek, one who is sent is an "apostle."

In other words, while they remain followers of Christ and continue to learn from him (to be disciples), they now have an additional role to play—a role given to them by Christ. These particular disciples are being commissioned to serve as ambassadors, legates, *apostles* of Christ. They are not merely to teach *about* Christ in some kind of academic or intellectualized way. Rather, they are to "make disciples" by introducing new followers to the very person of Christ the Master and his commands to love God and each other.

When we consider how the Church speaks about ordained ministry, including that of deacons, as a participation in *apostolic* ministry, we can only come to one conclusion: we are disciples (and we remain disciples, always learning from Christ!) who have also been sent out to make more disciples, teaching, serving, and introducing others to Christ Himself. It is not only various ecclesial documents (such as the *Catechism*) that use this language about deacons. In his 2000 address to deacons and their families in Rome on the occasion of the Jubilee Day for Deacons, Saint John Paul II referred to deacons as apostles:

> The Jubilee is an important time for self-examination and inner purification, but also for recovering that missionary awareness inherent in the mystery of Christ and the Church. Whoever believes that Christ the Lord is the way, the truth and the life, whoever knows that the Church is his continuation in history, whoever has a

personal experience of all this cannot fail, for this very reason, to become fervently missionary. Dear deacons, be active apostles of the new evangelization. Lead everyone to Christ! Through your efforts, may his kingdom also spread in your family, in your workplace, in the parish, in the Diocese, in the whole world!

Apostleship and Ministerial Identity

Earlier, speaking of our baptisms, I referred to a "theological reference point" offered by the Congregation for Catholic Education concerning deacons. Let me cite it again here: "First of all we must consider the diaconate, like every other Christian identity, from within the Church which is understood as a mystery of Trinitarian communion in missionary tension." With baptism, we focused on the mystery of Trinitarian communion; now, we find ourselves, especially in the words of Saint John Paul II, returning to the language of mission and "missionary tension."

I have often pondered the meaning of the expression "missionary tension." To have a mission seems rather easy to understand and identify, but what is this "missionary tension" all about, and how does it affect our ministerial identity as deacons? It seems to be that, as disciples of Christ, we often find ourselves immersed in our own relationship with Christ. This is not a bad thing! Consider the famous scene of the Transfiguration, where Peter is so overwhelmed by Christ that he wants to build tents and set up camp on the mountaintop. How often might we find ourselves with a similar response? We simply want to rest in the Lord on the mountaintop and let the rest of the world go on by, along the roads below.

Here's where the tension comes in. Christ rejects Peter's offer and challenges Peter, James, and John to leave the mountain and return to their responsibilities below. In fact, Christ Himself acknowledges that he cannot remain there either, but must go up to Jerusalem to complete his own mission, to suffer, to die, and to rise.

So, who are we, then, as deacons of Christ? We are disciples who are also now apostles with a mission. We are people who may not simply revel in our relationship with Christ and ignore the commission we have been given. We are people who leave security behind and strike out boldly ("Go into the deep!" says Christ), risking everything for the sake of the Gospel. This relationship between our discipleship, on the one hand, and our apostleship, on the other, is critical for understanding our diaconal ministerial identity. As disciples, we must, of course, remain connected with Christ, our Master (Teacher) and Lord; as "active apostles of the New Evangelization," we leave the security of our "classroom" and pour ourselves out in service to Christ, just as Christ did, Himself.

Perhaps the best example of this "missionary tension" is found in John's Gospel, when Jesus washes the feet of his *disciples* (cf. John 13). As Christ is washing their feet, a task that even a slave could not be ordered to perform, Peter initially objects. Jesus tells Peter that, if he wishes to remain in fellowship with him, he must do this, and Peter changes course immediately! Then, after he is finished, Jesus returns to his place at the table and asks them if they know what he has just done for them. Of course, they don't. Jesus explains: "I have given you a model to follow." Here's where things get very interesting.

Scripture scholars tell us that the word attributed to Jesus for "model" or "example" is the Greek word *hypodeigma*. Found only in this passage of the New Testament, this word is not simply any kind of model. It is specifically a model of how one is going to die. What Christ is teaching his followers is so much more than simple menial service! He is telling them that he is about to give his very life for them, and they, if they truly would follow him and lead others, must be prepared to do the same.

Our ministerial identity as deacons, then, challenges us to always remain faithful disciples of Christ, while also eagerly accepting the challenge of a kenotic apostleship. Our mission is to empty ourselves (*kenosis*) just as Christ has, to leave the comfort and security of the mountaintop for the rigors and messiness of life below, even to the point of giving our lives for others in imitation of Christ, our Master.

For Reflection

1. In my own spiritual life, how do I balance discipleship and apostleship?
2. How *kenotic* (self-emptying) is my approach to ministry?
3. Am I an "active apostle" leading everyone to Christ?

Notes

[12] Matthew 28:18-20 (NRSV).

Chapter IV

Deacons and Their States of Life: The Context of Identity

In 1967, when Pope Paul VI renewed the diaconate as an order permanently exercised in the Latin Church with the promulgation of *Sacrum Diaconatus Ordinem*, the experience of most Latin Catholics was with the celibate priesthood. When I entered high school seminary in 1963, the attitude was that we were beginning a journey that would lead to a clear choice: either we would proceed to ordination and a life of celibacy, or we would leave the seminary and eventually marry and raise a family. It was an either/or proposition. The relationship between "being ordained" and a celibate state of life seemed strong and almost unbreakable.

I say "almost" because of an event that took place at our central-Illinois parish when I was in parochial grade school. Like most of the boys in our school above a certain age, I was an altar server. One day, Sister came into the classroom and announced that the following week a priest of the Maronite (Catholic) Church was going to be coming for a visit. She mentioned that we would celebrate the Eucharist with him, but it would be celebrated in the Maronite Rite, which was considerably different from what we were used to. Immediately, every altar server in the room raised his hand. "Can I serve?" "Can I serve?"… We all wanted to be involved in this novel experience. Sister's answer was stunning. "No, you can't. Father's own sons will be serving with him."

His *what*? How could a priest have sons? Sister then patiently—and with considerable amusement at our shock—explained that Father was visiting from Lebanon and that, in the Eastern Catholic Churches, priests were often married men with families. Later on, while we were at the Maronite Divine Liturgy, most of us were watching Father and his sons move around the altar, simply wondering how a priest could be both priest and a family man at the same time. One of my friends later went to Sister and asked her repeatedly to reassure him that Father was, indeed, a Catholic priest! He just couldn't seem to wrap his mind around the possibility that being ordained and being married were not mutually exclusive.

In this chapter, then, we want to reflect upon the "states of life" which form the context from and within which we live out our ministerial identity as disciple and apostle. In Church documents, the term "state of life" refers generally to whether one is married, celibate, professed (into religious life), or widowed. In the 1998 *Basic Norms for the Formation of Permanent Deacons* from the Congregation for Catholic Education, we read:

> Obviously such a spirituality [of service] must integrate itself harmoniously, in each case, with the spirituality related to the state of life. Accordingly, the same diaconal spirituality acquires diverse connotations according to whether it be lived by a married man, a widower, a

single man, a religious, or a consecrated person in the world.[13]

Someone might ask why I did not include the Sacrament of Matrimony in the earlier chapter on sacramental foundations for ministry, specifically, the Sacraments of Initiation and Sacrament of Orders. Frequently in conversation, married deacons will refer to the "dual sacramentality" of the diaconate as they experience it, and the two sacraments are Matrimony and Holy Orders. I am trying to approach this question a bit differently.

The foundations of a ministerial identity of service are ultimately found in Initiation and Orders; these are the sacraments that call us to *ecclesial* service, regardless of our state of life. In other words, there is no sacramental difference between a celibate deacon and a married deacon. Both are deacons in precisely the same way. I was once asked to address the deacon candidates of a large Eastern archdiocese along with their wives. As I was waiting in the wings, a candidate walked up to me and, in an aggressive tone, told me he hoped that I was not going to "stand up here and talk about the wonderful married diaconate, and how it's so great that deacons and their wives form a ministerial team for the Church." I was pretty taken aback, but I told him I hadn't planned to talk about that, but why was he so angry? He calmed down and told me that over the previous years of formation, every teacher, retreat master, and guest speaker had talked incessantly about "the married diaconate." The problem was that this candidate was unmarried and would soon be making his solemn promise of perpetual celibacy. What he said next stunned me. "I have come to accept that, in the eyes of many people, I will always be a second-class deacon because I do not have a wife to bring with me."

The majority of deacons live and serve within the context of the Sacrament of Matrimony. Still, we cannot let the numbers alone create a sense that this is the only way in which diaconate may be lived. For example, I recall receiving a call from a man interested in the diaconate, but he told me that he was not qualified. When I asked him why not, he said that he was not married and he knew that you had to be married in order to be ordained a deacon!

The question we need to ponder, then, is not the "either/or" question of matrimony or ordination; but, rather, the question is one of integration: how do we integrate our baptismal and ordained identity as servants in and for the Church within our particular state of life, whatever that may be? We need to respect those "diverse connotations" referred to in the *Basic Norms* referenced above.

The *National Directory* on the diaconate offers words of encouragement and integration to deacons serving in several states of life: married life, celibate chastity, widowhood, and even those rare occasions when a deacon's family is experiencing divorce.[14] There is also a section on the fact that "in one way or another, celibacy affects every deacon, married or unmarried."[15]

For the married deacon and his family, the *Catechism* gives a wonderful insight. Namely that both sacraments—Matrimony and Holy Orders—are sacraments "at the service of Communion," and that in both of these sacraments of vocation, the focus is on "the other" in the relationship (cf. section 2, chapter 3). Husbands and wives live lives of complete service for and to each other: we give ourselves totally and perpetually to our spouses. The ordained are also focused outward, not on our own good and salvation, but for the good and salvation of others in the person of Christ and in the name of the Church. When both sacraments are joined together, as in the family life of a married deacon, this integration and outward focus takes on a powerful significance, both for the family and for the world around them. The graces of each sacrament assist the family in countless ways.

The celibate deacon lives out his ministerial identity with a particular focus and emphasis. Obviously, within the Latin Church, we have had greater experience with a celibate clergy, although a celibate permanent deacon is still living a state of life that is distinct from that of a celibate priest. The deacon is still working at a secular job or profession and may have other professional and personal obligations outside the Church. Still, while celibacy itself is not a sacrament in its own right, it provides the deacon with a context which encourages a single-minded emphasis on the needs of others, rather than his own.

A widowed deacon enters into a new relationship with others, as well. No longer married and expected to live now as a celibate man, the widower encounters a new pattern of life. He may still have family obligations and, at the same time, his relationships with other clergy and friends will enter a new phase which will affect how he lives out his service.

It was not the intent of this brief reflection to offer an extended discussion of the relationship of Matrimony or celibacy to the Sacrament of Holy Orders. My point is that the sacramental foundations of our ministerial identity rest with Initiation into discipleship and Ordination into apostleship. These sacraments constitute and establish our ministerial identity *as deacons*. However, that identity is then lived out within a particular life context, and this is where these various "states of life" come in. A deacon is a deacon is a deacon. However, how that deacon lives out the details and demands of this ministry will be profoundly and substantively affected by his state of life.

> ### *For Reflection*
> 1. What is your state of life? In what specific ways has your state of life affected your own identity as a deacon, as well as the actual exercise of diaconate?
> 2. How might your state of life change in the future? The U.S. bishops caution that a widowed deacon may not normally remarry (since an ordained person incurs an impediment to enter Matrimony); how does such a reality affect your own life and ministry?

Notes

[13] Congregation for Catholic Education, *Basic Norms for the Formation of Permanent Deacons* (Vatican City: Libreria Editrice Vaticana, 1998), #12.

[14] United States Conference of Catholic Bishops, *The National Directory for the Formation, Ministry and Life of Permanent Deacons in the United States* (Washington, DC: USCCB, 2004), #66-76.

[15] Ibid., #72.

Chapter V

Ministerial Identity: It's All About Relationships

When all is said and done, the ministerial identity of the deacon is all about relationships. The Congregation for the Clergy, in its 1998 *Directory for the Ministry and Life of Permanent Deacons*, writes that:

> By a special sacramental gift, Holy Order confers on the deacon a particular participation in the consecration and mission of Him who became servant of the Father for the redemption of mankind, and inserts him in a new and specific way in the mystery of Christ, of his Church and the salvation of all mankind. Hence the spiritual life of the deacon should deepen this threefold relationship by developing *a*

[SPIRITUAL LIFE OF A DEACON SHOULD DEEPEN INTO A] community spirituality which bears witness to that communion essential to the nature of the Church. [emphasis added][16]

I find that expression "a community spirituality" to be especially helpful. Building on what was said in the last chapter, the ministerial identity of the deacon, regardless of his state of life, is outwardly focused on "the other." By stressing a community spirituality, we see the same kind of outward focus. In this chapter, let's consider some of the relationships we nurture as part of our ministerial identity and spirituality.

The *Directory* properly cites our relationship with Christ as the primary relationship we are to have and to nurture. In a particular way, we have a relationship with the kenotic Christ, who emptied himself in the service of others. Because of our relationship with Christ, and within the Trinitarian life we share from baptism, we are in relationship with "the Church." In virtue of our ordination, that relationship with the Church is deepened. We are now called to serve that communion and to act in its name as an ordained minister of the Church.

Before going on with other specific relationships, let's talk about the relationship we have with the three-fold ministry of Word, Sacrament, and Charity/Justice. Our sacramental identity is expressed in the balanced exercise of these ministry, not one over against the others. As the bishops of the United States have consistently reminded us, there is an "inherent unity" between and among these three areas, and we need to keep in mind that the sacramental power of the diaconate is found precisely in this balanced exercise.

I have often spoken of the diaconate as a ministry of "connecting the dots." When people encounter us, they should be able to experience a confluence of meaning: how the proclamation of Christ (the Word) leads us to worship and praise (Sacrament), which in turn leads us to work for Charity and Justice. We must have a relationship with each and all of these functions so that we can truly be sacramental icons of *diakonia*.

While not a relationship brought into existence through ordination, our relationship with our spouses (if married) and families (celibates have families, too!) must also be nurtured and promoted. (This can certainly be extended to deacons who are members of religious communities, as well.) We live our ministerial identity at all times, and not simply when vested or involved in some work at church.

As we learned from St. John Paul II, one of the reasons for renewing the diaconate was to inject the Church's sacred ministers into new areas, and one of the areas he mentions is the family. In other words, after ordination, we are deacon *to* and *for* our families, as well. That means so much more than that we perform all the family's baptisms, weddings, and funerals! It means that our familial relationships are the subject and object of our concern, care, and love, both as husbands, fathers, sons, uncles, and cousins, but also as deacons.

Among the ecclesial relationships established through ordination, our relationship with the bishop is right at the top. In fact, the *National Directory* on the diaconate offers an excellent overview of these relationships, beginning with the bishop. In our ministry of service, the deacon has—from the beginning of the diaconate—been linked to the ministry of the bishop. It is the bishop alone who ordains us for service in the first place, and our task is to extend the bishop's care and concern into areas he might not normally be able to reach. Through our promise of obedience and the relationship established at ordination, we become closely associated with the bishop.

I was ordained some months ahead of my formation class because I was being sent to a new assignment by the US Navy; the Cardinal agreed to ordain me before I left. As a result, I got his undivided attention throughout the ceremony! After the Prayer after Communion, the Cardinal asked the assembly to be seated. He thanked everyone for coming and those who had organized the beautiful liturgy. He then said that he knew many people in attendance, including Catholics, might not fully appreciate the new relationship he now shared with me, his newest deacon. "On days of special joy, such as this ordination, the Church asks bishops to wear—under the chasuble of the priest"—and here he gathered up his chasuble in one hand—"the dalmatic of the deacon"—and, in his other hand, he raised up his dalmatic, which he was wearing under the chasuble. "This is how close Bill and I now are." It was a profoundly moving and meaningful moment of catechesis for all of us who experienced it.

As a result of our new relationship with the diocesan bishop, we enter into a new relationship with the whole diocesan Church. We now take on a share of the bishop's own responsibility for all people (and not just the Catholics) who live within the boundaries of the diocese. While we may be assigned for some ministries to a parish, our frame of reference must always transcend the parish and consider the entire diocese. Our ministerial identity is one of total service, and that service is not compartmentalized or restricted to some portion of the diocesan Church. We share in that diocesan-wide responsibility.

Upon ordination, we enter into the "Order of Deacons." Even when we are ordained all by ourselves (as I was), we are not "Lone Ranger" deacons. We become part of something larger than ourselves—the whole Order of Deacons around the world. In terms of ministerial identity, we should foster communion within and among the diaconate. Beyond this, however, I think we should also find ways of ministering collaboratively on various pastoral projects. There is, truly, "power in numbers" and to have a team of deacons collaborating in service can be a particularly powerful sign of the Church's own servant-identity.

We also enter into a new relationship with the presbyterate, of course. As brothers in ministry, we work together for the good of all. Perhaps our closest ministerial partners on a daily basis, presbyters need our assistance to fully appreciate the ways in which deacons in their own right can and should contribute to the pastoral care of parishioners. We must do all we can to foster and nurture this fraternal relationship. One pastor with whom I served once told me how much he appreciated the diaconate. "I was raised on a farm, and from an early age I valued the work of a team: different people with different gifts working together for a common goal. That's how I look at us! Priests and deacons do different things and in different ways, but when we're all pulling together, it's a wonderful thing!"

We also enter into new ministerial relationships with religious women and men. I recall a conversation I had with the superior of a convent outside of Budapest, who remarked to our group that "sisters and deacons are natural collaborators. We're both about 'service' for others. Sisters and deacons are truly brothers and sisters!" As deacons, we must be aware of the particular charisms associated with various congregations and religious orders and do all we can to support and extend their ministries.

With regard to our new relationship with the laity in general, it is essential to remember where we started this reflection on ministerial identity: it all starts with Baptism! The laity with whom we serve have their own vocational call to service within the Church and within the world. Our task is not to try to do those things in their stead, and the laity are not simply "recipients" of the ministries we "provide." Baptized disciples share in the life and ministry of the Church in their own right, and we are ministers of empowerment, helping them as we can to live out the demands of their own various vocations.

Finally, we enter into a new relationship with society as a whole. Our identity as deacons of the Church gives us a particular leadership role in evangelizing society and in seeking the common good of all, even outside the boundaries of the Church. We become, in effect, official spokespersons for the Church in many contexts, and our prophetic voice—heard in many different contexts because of our living and working within secular society—can be an effective witness of Christ and His love for all.

In short, our ministerial identity is all about relationships. As a servant, our attention is always directed toward our Lord and to those we serve: family, friends, work, school, parish, hospital, prison, and on and on and on. Our identity is characterized by this constant outreach to the Other. A servant who quits attending to others, and focuses only on his own concerns, quickly ceases being a servant at all! By baptism and ordination, and from within our particular states of life, we constantly turn outward, extending the Good News of Christ to the world around us.

> *For Reflection*
> 1. Which relationships in my life and ministry right now need the most attention?
> 2. Which relationships in my life and ministry right now give me the most inspiration and motivation?
> 3. Are there areas in which I do not yet have a particular relationship? What might I do to establish one?

Notes

[16] Congregation for the Clergy, *Directory for the Ministry and Life of Permanent Deacons* (Vatican City: Libreria Editrice Vaticana), #46.

Deacon William T. Ditewig, Ph.D., directs the offices of faith formation, permanent diaconate, and pastoral planning for the Diocese of Monterey, California. A frequent contributor to *Deacon Digest Magazine*, he is a prolific author, adjunct professor of theology, and a theological consultant. Former executive director of the Secretariat for the Diaconate at the USCCB, Deacon Ditewig is a retired commander in the United States Navy.